SUMMARY:

We're Going To Need More Wine

Stories That Are Funny, Complicated, and True

ABBEY BEATHAN

Copyright

The names and identifying characteristics of many of the individuals featured throughout this book have been changed to protect their privacy. In some cases, composite characters have been created or timelines have been compressed, in order to further preserve privacy and to maintain narrative flow. The goal in all cases was to protect people's privacy without damaging the integrity of the story.

WE'RE GOING TO NEED MORE WINE.

FIRST EDITION

Print ISBN: 978-0-06-269398-3 (Hardcover)

Print ISBN: 978-0-06-283559-8 (B&N BF Signed Edition)

Print ISBN: 978-0-06-283561-1 (BAM Signed Edition)

EPub Edition October 2017 ISBN 978-0-06-269400-3

Table of Contents

The Book at a Glance

In the twelfth chapter of this book, author, actress, and stepmother extraordinaire Gabrielle Union writes about the speech she delivered for Essence magazine on being "Fierce and Fearless", in which she talked about the pretending, fearing, and hiding she had been doing in her life. Oprah Winfrey was one of the audience members who were left awestricken at the end of her speech, saying she had never heard anyone be that honest, in public or in private.

This moment she writes about in the book is important because it highlights what the book is about, at its core: honesty. Complete, unfazed, almost drunken honesty. From the very beginning of her book, the introduction page, Union writes that if ever the reader didn't agree with what she was imparting in her stories, they could at least commend her honesty. In this book, she leaves out nothing of her journey. She writes about hiding under the bed at a particular low point in life, and having her dog lay next to her just to make it okay. She writes about standing up for her son after the school administrators called him a bully, armed with reference books on black oppression to teach the school a lesson. She writes about sex, heartbreak, marriage, trauma, and death --- some stories funny, and others determined to leave the readers with something to put in their back pocket for when they find themselves in the exact same place.

Apart from honesty, one other thing to expect from this book is Union's consistency. Throughout her stories, she never forgets herself. As a proud black woman who grew up with issues of race constantly being left out of the conversation, and witnesses it happen to this day, she is consistent in making the connection between her experiences and her blackness, because she believes no amount of success or 'making it' ever makes any black person immune from the issues their people face on a daily basis. She is consistent in that she learns from all the experiences she shares in this book, and she is consistent in the way she grows from these mistakes. As a child, Union tried her best to escape from her blackness by trying to be known for anything but her color. Even though she attributes her success now to being touched by the hearts of her people, she does not leave this out because it was a part of her learning. And landmarks of her learning are consistent throughout her stories.

At the end of the day, these stories are stories of learning, or rather, these stories create a cycle of learning. Union writes about what she has learned from the people she has met in life, and from her own experiences. In turn, the lessons she imparts from these stories are opportunities for her reader to learn as well. Her stories are an invitation for the reader to learn more about their own lives, and learn how much other people can learn from their lives all the same.

Introduction

"This kind of feels like a first date", the author writes to start off the introduction to her book of stories. By writing this, she likens the feeling of beginning to write this book to the anxiety and excitement that comes with embarking on a journey towards intimacy with a stranger. But it is exactly this intimacy that the author wishes to share with her reader, painting the image of close friends exchanging crazy stories at a restaurant while asking the waiter to pour more wine in between bouts of laughter and tears.

She speaks to the reader directly when she recounts small moments over the course of her writing, such as leafing through some of her own favorite books. The author highlights a favorite phrase from writer James Baldwin, which read *"The very time I thought I was lost, My dungeon shook and my chains fell off."* It is here that the author begins to write about the dungeons of her past, and the sensation of being held back by the chains of self-identity issues and growing up in Hollywood. She writes about those who rescued her from these dungeons, and finally, she speaks of how she eventually had to *'shake off her own shackles'*, as she puts it, by learning to choose herself.

Nearing the end of her introduction, the author returns to the analogy of the first date, and reminds the reader of the presence of trust issues on the threshold of every relationship. She writes that she hopes her readers do not doubt her intentions, and at the very least, appreciate her honesty. Finally, she writes about one other thing that comes with sharing one's stories with the world: the fear of having to revisit them in one's own head. The author writes that while it had been difficult at first, she eventually viewed the experience as a way to find her 'authentic self', a step towards accepting what has been her life and what is to come. Quoting Carrie Fisher, she admits that she is afraid, but she is brave enough to do it anyway.

1: Ladies and Gentlemen, Miss Pleasanton

The author begins this first story with a passage written by W.E.B. Du Bois, which highlighted the conflicting duality of being a Negro in America, in that a Black person must always see themselves 'through the eyes of others', and decide which they want to be first: an American or a Negro. This passage and its message would be relevant to the writer's early life, which she writes about in this chapter.

When she was in the second grade, the author and her family moved from Omaha, Nebraska, a city with an expansive black community, to Pleasanton, California, wherein their family would be in the author's words, *'the chocolate chip in the cookie'*. Being the only black girl in her school initially, the author recalls the first time a classmate called her a 'nigger', and the nickname 'Nigger Nickie' caught on. Following this, the author wrote about eventually dedicating all her efforts to being 'less black', careful not to fall into Black stereotypes doing her best to excel in school.

When another black girl started attending her school and was ridiculed by most, the author recounts making it a point to not associate with her. The author sums up what she had felt at the time by writing, *"I was afraid to take the risk of being black by standing next to her."*

Besides being smart, the author felt during her childhood that, for the sake of a sense of safety, she also had to be popular. She recalls doing impressions of Buckwheat, a black character on Saturday Night Live at her friends' request, because she had the same unruly hair. The author realizes, in her writing, that if she were as proud of her blackness back then as she was now, she wouldn't have taken the directives, and *'they wouldn't know what to do with her'*.

During the later period of her childhood, the author writes about how she and her friends had experimented with drinking; they had stolen a keg, conned their way into getting money for alcohol, and played fun drinking games. It was within these drinking circles, where friends would throw the word 'nigger' around without realizing she was there, that she learned there was a difference between 'niggers' and 'cool black people', and that most of her friends knew her as the latter. She recalls a similar situation in which her classmates were surprised one of their 'cool' friends was a Jew. She knows this as a testament to how the minorities in Pleasanton did all they could to blend in, because it was the only way they would be considered equal.

When the author was thirteen, she began to spend her summers back in Omaha to spend time with her grandmother. In Omaha, she became a part of her cousin Kenyatta's social circle. The author writes, *"She had all these tough friends, some of whom had already been to juvie. They were all pretty and all having sex."* Through this group of black teenagers and the experience of living in a black community again, the author writes that she *'relearned blackness'*. The author recalls the slow atmosphere of their Omaha neighborhood begin to change, as drugs became easier to come around, and as people she was close with got involved in the business. Soon, her friends began to join gangs, gain power, and eventually become wealthy. The author writes that she had not viewed crack as a bad thing initially, because her friends were finally making a living.

As the gang situation escalated in Omaha, however, the danger became apparent to the author. She recalls hiding her cousin's boyfriend, who was wanted for a drive-by shooting, in the basement for weeks, until he turned himself in. Along with him, she recounts what had happened to various other friends, all of whom had gotten mixed up with gangs of some sort, and because of it, went to prison or was killed.

In comparing the way she acted in the tough Omaha neighborhood to how quickly she reverted to being *'the invisible black girl'* once back in Pleasanton, the author realized that she, and many other African Americans, were caught in what she calls a *'dual consciousness'*, or the constant attempt to fulfill what it is to be American and what it is to be Negro at the same time, in the same body. The author ends the first story by recognizing how exhausting of a feat it is, and apologizing to her younger self for not seeing how amazing she was from the start.

2: Sex Miseducation

In this chapter, the author writes about the period in her life wherein her and her other girlfriends first began to learn about their bodies and explore their sexuality. Here, the author writes about her first menstrual period, finding out where her vagina is, and how girls learned about sex and sexuality before the age of the internet. Through the telling of her crazy experiences, the author not only shows her readers what it means to be a young girl, but rather she reminds her readers of their own stories of friendship, discovery, and adventure.

The author begins the chapter by looking back at a Sex Education session she attended in the fifth grade, where the only knowledge truly imparted to them was that once their menstruation began, they could get pregnant at any moment. Not being told much by anyone else, the author and her friends first found what they needed to know in the pages of a Judy Blume book. She recalled the moment a girl in her class became the first to have her period, and the lingering fear that came with being the next one. Soon enough, the author got 'it' at a Macy's bathroom, and, with the help of her friends, became a woman. The author writes about the fear continuing, with the uncertainty of the next period, and the accidents that might follow if one would guess wrong.

The author also talks about her first experiences with masturbation. She recalls having initially thought that her clitoris *was* her vagina, and how it took a period emergency during a swimming day, a tampon, and a supportive friend for her to find out that it really wasn't. The author knew that the reason for her cluelessness was society's unwillingness to talk about things they thought made others uncomfortable.

Following this, the author writes about sex. If Judy Blume had not only been their reference text for menstruation --- she was also their guide to the before, during, and after, of sex. She looks back at the moment her friend told their friend group that she was pregnant, after having unprotected sex at a party. Their entire group scrounged up money to pay for an abortion. At the abortion clinic, the author recalls taking a box of condoms, and eventually giving condoms out at parties.

Finally, the author compares how she and her friends approached sex back then, to how teenagers do nowadays. She writes about teaching the teenagers of today about reciprocation, or asking from the other person what you had just given. *"I WANT PEOPLE TO MAKE INFORMED,*

JOYFUL CHOICES ABOUT SEX." she writes, as she continues to write about the beauty of not viewing sex as taboo, but rather enjoying it and exploring new ways to do it, shamelessly and without giving too much thought about society's expectations. She concludes the chapter by asking the readers to make a promise to themselves: that they will learn about their body, use it freely, enjoy what it can be used for, and share what they learn with others. In the author's words, *"So help me Judy Blume."*

3: Black Girl Blues

In this chapter, the author tackles the common insecurities that black men and women have about their physical appearance, such as their skin, hair and nose. She begins the chapter by recounting an encounter with a young boy who stayed under the shade during a race because he didn't want to get any more black. The experience reminded the author of how obsessed she also was with light skin as a child, having been raised to believe light skin equaled beauty, both among her peers and her own black family. The author recalled how her light-skinned mother had never praised her for her beauty, but wrote that she later realized the reason why. Her mother didn't want to raise her believing looks would get her to where she wanted to be in life.

Aside from her skin, the author was also insecure about her Afro hair growing up. She remembers convincing her mother to drive her to a salon, wherein she would get her hair straightened with 'relaxer', a hair treatment containing harsh chemicals. During one relaxer session, the author recalls not telling her hairdresser that her scalp was burning, because she had wanted the relaxer to stay on for longer. Hair problems hit deeper for the author than most. She writes, *"At twelve, I had not been once called pretty. Not by friends, not by my family, and certainly not by boys. My friends all had people checking them out and had their isn't-that cute elementary school boyfriends. I was completely and utterly alone and invisible."*

Once she began her career in Hollywood, the author experienced an entirely new variety of hair issues, in that most Hollywood hair and makeup artists, who are most often white, did not know how to properly style black hair. The author talks about the decision to grow out her relaxed hair and wear weaves instead, and eventually, the decision to wear wigs. She writes that while she decided to switch from natural hair for ease and practicality, especially in her career, she still felt unease. *"Does this wig mean I'm not comfortable in my blackness? If I wear my hair natural, do I somehow become more enlightened?"* she asks herself. Even when it came to other hair decisions, like going blond or even choosing to wear natural hair for a change, everyone always had something to say. In the end, all of these experiences led her to a single realization: that no matter how strongly people ascribed characteristics to girls with certain types of hair, it would never be a basis of how good of a person they are.

Finally, the author writes about her nose. Growing up, the author recalls pinching her nose with a clothespin or even contorting her face in a way that would make her nose seem thinner. And as an actress, she recounts receiving backlash for a nose job she never had done. At the end of the chapter of talking about big insecurities, she simply shrugs and writes, '*Maybe one day, when I'm a real grown-up, I will wear my hair natural and I won't contour my nose. Hell, I'll just be me. And hopefully people will accept me the way I am.*"

4: The Ballad of Nickie and Little Screw

In this chapter, the author writes about a boy named Billy Morrison, the truck she wanted her name to be etched onto so badly, her first sexual experience, and the feeling of being wanted.

The author recalls the time when scraggly haired, crooked toothed Billy, who was nicknamed "Little Screw", moved into Pleasanton and started to attend her school. While all of the girls were fascinated by his appearance, the author remembers being more in love than anyone, after hearing rumors that he had 'dated a black girl' in his old town. This was an important moment for the author, because as a black girl in a town full of conservatives, boys never considered her to even be an option. Even the two African American boys, she writes, would steer clear of her, just as she would with them, for fear of being 'superbrown'.

Because Billy was a baseball player and the author played softball, the author's only encounters with him were brief, and often at the park, after playing their respective games. Despite this, and even as Billy started dating a Mexican girl, the author believed she had a chance. Finally, he invited her to hang out, and brought her to his parents' room. The author writes, *"Holy shit, I remember thinking, I'm so not supposed to be in here. We're in here and we're going to fuck."* She then retells the event of losing her virginity, as she remembers being scared of him seeing 'a black pussy', bleeding on the sheets, and feeling disappointed at the lack of romance that came with the experience.

Billy had gotten back with his girlfriend shortly after their hook-up, but the author shares it had not been their last, writing that while she was dating other guys, she would cheat with Billy every now and then. Earlier in the chapter, the author describes vividly Billy's GMC truck, which had his name boldly written on the back. At the end of the chapter, the author writes that her name would never be right next to his.

5: Open House

In this chapter, the author writes about her mother, her father, and their divorce in her senior year of college. She writes about why her mother had chosen to stay quiet about her father's affair, and how she and her sister had handled the discovery.

She begins the chapter by writing about something her mother loved to do: attend art events in neighboring towns and start a conversation with a stranger. The author attributes this to the fact that her mother was bored in Pleasanton, especially since her husband was absent most of the time. She recalls how her father had stopped funding her mother's master's education, after he finally found out her course, an arts course, would not help her get promoted in her telecommunications job.

Following this, she looks back at the moment she and her sister began to unravel the truth about his other woman. She had discovered a separate ATM card in her father's drawer, and her sister confirmed the rest, having seen photos of their father and the other woman on several vacation trips. This was how they pieced together that he had been lying about his whereabouts for years. Once, out of anger, the author recalls deliberately losing a soccer match, and watching her father yell ‘choke’ along with a sea of white faces. For the first time, she swore at her father.

During their last few years of marriage, the author’s parents never spoke to each other. But she retells the story of how her mother had seen two tickets for a ballet show, and had gotten ready for a date, only to watch her husband pick up the tickets and leave. Later on, she would tell her daughter that those tickets weren’t the first she expected to have been for her, but that she endured it, because she didn’t want to disrupt their comfortable life. Soon, her father would want her mother out of the picture, but she wouldn’t go.

Finally, she writes about the night everything came to an end. After the author and her younger sister had gotten into a fight with their father, he left angrily and left a note to his wife with her name misspelled. And her mother had written a note back, saying she was leaving him. Her father and his other woman would go on to get married --- she and her sisters all attended the wedding --- and her mother moved back to Omaha.

The author brings this story to a close by sharing with the readers what her mother did after retiring. She had helped out a relative with a drug problem by taking in her three newborn children. At seventy, the author writes, her mother still does everything she can to raise the children right.

6: Who Hates You Most?

In this chapter, the author shares with her readers the story of how she became the target of a girl's furious quest for revenge. The title she chose for this chapter was inspired by a game she and her costars played while they were stuck in the conference room of a movie set, wherein they each told the story of who hated them most. The author had easily won the game by telling them about her insane encounters with a girl named Queeshaun.

The author had started dating future basketball star Jason Kidd in her junior year of high school, but first met Jason when he was still dating a girl named Angela, who was also a basketball player like the author. Little did the author know, her new boyfriend's then-girlfriend happened to have a very protective best friend.

She first met Queeshaun at a high school pep rally. Queeshaun had barged into the event and came charging at her saying "I'm gonna whoop yo' ass, bitch!" After getting dragged out by security, she promised to return.

Soon, Queeshaun began leaving threats on her family's answering machine, and her father had no choice but to bring it up with the police, who only laughed at Queeshaun's choice of words. The author saw her worst nightmare again at a basketball game against Queeshaun's best friend Angela, but this time, her older sister Kelly walked into the gymnasium and threatened Queeshaun just as bad.

Finally, on the last day of her junior year, Queeshaun appeared once more. She had stuck her hand into the window of the car the author and her friends were in, and attempted to grab the author out of the car. As they drove forward to escape, Queeshaun ran after them, and somehow managed to get back up after a hard fall. Eventually, they outsmarted her and sought refuge in a house party.

Years later, the author writes, she met Angela's younger brother at university, and she had asked him if Angela blamed her for Jason Kidd breaking up with her. The brother said she didn't, then followed with, "But Queeshaun? That crazy bitch still talks about you."

7: Code 261

In this chapter, the author tells the story of the most traumatic experience of her life. She talks about how the experience continues to affect her daily life today, and how it has shaped her advocacies.

At nineteen years old during the summer after her freshman year of college, the author was working at a Payless store. There had been news about a number of Payless stores across the country being robbed by a former employee who was black. Despite this, the Payless store the author was working at sent no cautionary notices.

The author was working a night shift at the store with only one other employee when a black man walked in a few minutes before closing time. He had briefly asked the author about some shoes before holding up the counter. He took the few hundred dollars that were still in the register, and held the author and her co-worker at gunpoint. Next, he asked them to take off their clothes. He left the coworker in the bathroom, ordered the author to come out, and raped her with a gun to her head. The author writes that she began to *'hover over herself'*, watching the man do to a body what she never thought would happen to someone like her. Soon, the author got hold of the man's gun and attempted to shoot him, but missed. When the man eventually asked for the exit and left, she and the coworker called for help.

Along with several police officers, the author's father and older sister arrived at the crime scene. Her sister, a criminal justice student, recognized that Code 261 meant rape, and informed her father. The author writes that she could never forget the look on her father's face when he found out: *"It was as if someone had broken his favorite toy."* The author recalls that her mother was equally heartbroken, arriving at the realization that they had moved to an all-white community like Pleasanton to protect their daughters, but things like this could still happen.

After the incident, the author writes that her father attended every court hearing, walked through every legal step, and later on, handled the parole proceedings as well. To her father, the process was personal. He had taken offense at the fact that the rapist had even dared to take something precious of his: his favorite daughter.

The rapist accepted a plea deal and ended up getting a sentence of thirty-three years. She writes that people have asked her often about whether or not she wished she could have killed the rapist, to which she answers that she didn't think she could live with the trauma of having killed someone. In addition, she would often get asked what she was wearing, despite the obvious fact that she had been raped during a work shift.

For the rest of the chapter, the author talks about how the experience had affected her daily life, her perception of her environment, and her reaction to particular situations. *"Timing became the most important thing in my life. I timed everything I did to try to reduce the space for something else to happen to me."* she writes, adding that she became wary of being in places as mundane as restaurants and libraries, due to the fear of being held hostage, carjacked, or anything of the sort.

She also writes about her experience as a part of the UCLA Rape Crisis Center. Among everyone in the support group, she was the only one who had been raped by a stranger. The others had to come back to school and go to classes with their rapists. In the Rape Crisis Center, she felt her world expand again, as she met others who went through the same trauma but were slowly moving forward with their lives.

Finally, she shares with her readers how the incident is affecting her life 24 years later. She talks about the struggle of being heavily guarded due to a traumatic experience, and being famous at the same time. She writes that she can't remember the last time she went into a bank, and that she could never sit at a restaurant with her back to the door. Paparazzi and fans who have a tendency to crowd, prod and grab do not help either. She recalls a particular incident in Las Vegas, where a cheerleading team crowded around her and began to cheer, alluding to her role in the movie 'Bring It On', who she had waved off. She also cites a similar instance during a family brunch with her husband Dwyane Wade and their three sons, when an entire family came over to their table. Although she and her husband had politely declined to entertain the family, the mother grabbed her arm and hissed at her in irritation.

At the end of the chapter, the author writes about a more heartwarming incident in a women's bathroom. Having been a strong anti-rape advocate and sharing her story of being raped for the entirety of a career, other women tended to recognize her and what she has done. In the bathroom, a woman had told her *"Me, too."* She recalls that she and the woman had not extended any affection towards each other beyond a slight nod.

"We don't hug. We don't cry. She nods back at me.
Just two women in a moment of mutual respect,
acknowledging the truth and consequences of our experience.
Feeling, in that moment, less alone on our respective islands."

8: Black Woman Blues

The author begins this chapter with a phrase she has been hearing her entire life: *"You know, you are really pretty for a dark-skinned girl."* Here, she writes about the ubiquitous presence of colorism, a term for holding lighter skinned African Americans to a higher regard than those with darker skin, both within black culture and society in general. She writes about how her dark skin has been constantly equated with her beauty and worth throughout her life, and how she fell into this trap herself growing up.

At the start of the chapter, the author cites particular instances wherein strangers or acquaintances would marvel at how attractive she was despite being dark-skinned. She then began to talk about her own resentment towards girls with light skin growing up. She felt especially threatened by light skinned girls whom she felt would steal boys' attention away from her. Despite this, her light-skinned mother had also experienced her fair share of hate and discrimination from dark-skinned girls, who called her 'piss colored'.

Describing her conversation with a younger dark skinned friend, the author expresses the fallacy of the saying, "Love the skin you're in", for it was being tossed around in a world where darker skin literally put you at a disadvantage. Research on colorism showed that lighter skinned women made approximately twenty-six hundred dollars more in a year than darker skinned women, and were also more likely to marry high status men. However, while they are undermined by men and most of society, the author also writes that darker skin becomes fetishized as well, especially after stars like Lupita Nyong'o became bigger names in the industry.

The author writes about firsthand experiences with being rejected by darker skinned men, simply because they wanted to 'lighten their gene pool'. She cites this instances to further show that even dark skinned men are 'color struck', in that they feel their children have a better shot at success if they are born with lighter skin.

She talks about being 'color struck' in her own way growing up, and how she only dated men with lighter skin than hers. This was first pointed out to her during a lunch conversation with an old friend. The conversation helped her realize that she only dated particular men not because she preferred lighter skin, but rather because she was fixated on men with lighter skin preferring *her*. After this realization, she began to start dating men in all varieties. She writes that finally dating black men helped her self-confidence as well, because she didn't have to endure the remarks of people who had a hard time believing a light skinned man would have his arm around a girl like her.

Following this, she writes about an experience in Vietnam, where she had asked a young girl why people were in public wearing surgical masks and long sleeved clothing despite the heat. The girl told her that being dark was associated with poverty, because it meant that one worked under the sun all day. She aligns this with how famous whitening creams are around the world, and how whitening advertisements are painful yet draw from reality, because fairer women *do* have a higher chance of getting men or jobs.

Finally, she writes about receiving another kind of twisted compliment many times in her life --- that she was really pretty for a black girl. This compliment would come not from other black people but from her white friends back in Pleasanton, who, to this day, still have very minimal interactions with other black people. She writes that the issue of colorism should be expanded beyond the black community, and in the end, should simply teach men and women to teach the men and women in their lives, that they are beautiful, not in spite of their features, but because of it.

9: Mistletoe Girl #2 Tells All

In this chapter, the author shares several stories about different experiences she has had throughout her acting career, such as interactions with fellow actors, relationships she built with her cast mates, and encounters with directors and other mentor figures on movie sets. In some of these experiences, she highlights how black actors and professionals, no matter how much they have accomplished, still have their credibility questioned by their peers.

She begins the chapter with her experience on the set of a movie called *Saved By The Bell: New Class,* where she made her film debut as 'Mistletoe Girl #2'. She writes that she enjoyed watching the main actors work on set, not only while shooting their scenes, but also with how they interacted with directors and co-stars. With every movie set she was on, she learned more by observing the actors she worked with. While on the set for one movie, an assistant director took a seat next to her and told her that he had two tips: first, that she should stop smiling too intently on set, and this: *'you are always going to be able to find people who don't want to watch you fail.'* She expresses that while Hollywood is often perceived as a ruthless industry, it was also where she met many genuine people who helped her in her career along the way.

She talks about the atmosphere of the auditions or casting calls she found herself in. While she was only doing it for herself, many others she came in contact with had families depending on them. She recalls talking to one guy, who she says is now a successful actor, whose family had been living out of their car and washing up when they got to the audition venue.

The author then writes about her tight bond with her cast mates during filming for 10 Things I Hate About You. She wrote about the skiing and camping trips they tool along the way, and about her friendship with Heath Ledger. She had gotten her younger cast mates fake IDs, gotten drunk and high with them, and generally just formed friendships that would last long after they wrapped shooting. She would go on to have good conversations with Heath Ledger every time they would see each other in Los Angeles, and writes, *"His loss was a death in the family that all of us felt equally."*

Next, she writes about her experiences on the set of 'Bring It On', where she played the role of Isis, the head cheerleader of a black cheer squad whose routine was stolen by a white cheerleading squad. In the original script of the movie, the author noticed that her character's lines were heavy with made-up slang which were perceived as typical for a black character. The author knew that Isis was a strong and educated girl however, so she worked with scriptwriters and directors to help make her character more real. When the film went on to be a cult classic, the author shared that she would often encounter fans who reenacted the cheers and lines from the films when they saw her, but would often say Isis' signature line *'It's been brought'* as *'It's been broughten'*, a line from another movie that spoofed Bring It On. She felt as though fans often mistook this as the real line because it ascribed better to Isis' identity as a black character.

Finally, she writes about her experience on the set of hit show Friends, where she played the role of a woman pursued by characters Joey and Ross at the same time. While shooting one of her scenes with the main Friends cast, she noticed how the director had blatantly changed his tone when talking to the main cast, and when talking to her. The director had given her instructions as if she were a toddler, she writes, even though she had more movies under her belt than some of the main cast members. At this point in friends, the author and Aisha Tyler, who played Ross' girlfriend Charlie Wheeler, had been the only two black actors with speaking lines in Friends. The whitewashing in Friends had only become apparent to the general public in 2016, and while the Friends creators assured they didn't intend for the show to be an all-white cast, the author expresses that the way the director had treated her was the reason they didn't have black talent on the show.

At the end of the chapter, she writes that the advice her parents had given her as a child was still relevant to her life as a grown woman. She had to be bigger, badder and better just to be considered equal.

10: Crash-and-Burn Marriage

In this chapter, the author writes about the beginning, middle and end of her marriage with former football player Chris ____. She goes through the entire journey, from meeting him at a party in college, marrying him shortly after, catching him cheating on several occasions, and finally deciding to go through with a divorce, after she had overcome her fear of being known as someone with a failed marriage.

She begins this chapter with excerpts from the day of her wedding. She recalls almost breaking out in tears as she walked down the aisle, not out of happiness, but out of fear for their future. As she walked up to him on the altar, the author remembers feeling afraid of Chris finding out about the cheating she had done herself, even though he was cheating even more. Describing the moment they were declared husband and wife, she writes, *"On the video, which I have watched only once, you see my face fall. It was the beginning of the end."*

She then returns to the story of how she and Chris first met. She had spotted him at a party hosted by his football teammates, and was intrigued by his frayed hems and Ducati. He showed interest throughout the trip, and began dating shortly after. When they started dating, the author recalls, Chris had told her he was planning to finish his kinesiology degree and get a career in sports medicine. He proposed to her after three months. She had said yes, mainly because most of her friends were already married at the time.

The author caught her new fiancée cheating only hours after they got engaged, when she saw a message from one of his friends about another girl. She had thrown his new engagement ring at him, as he begged and apologized relentlessly. However, the author was too afraid of being publicly humiliated to call off their marriage.

One year into their engagement, Chris was cut from the Jacksonville Jaguars, and was eventually cut from his new team, the Raiders, as well. After losing his source of income, the author began to pay for their living expenses as well as his own needs, such as a new office space for a company he planned in his head. At this point in their relationship, he was still cheating. Although most of the time the author wouldn't acknowledge it, evidence he left around triggered her jealousy. Other times, she would pull at all the stops to see if he would come to play the role of her husband, even faking an injury so that he would attend a movie premiere with her.

The author writes about their experience in couples' therapy.

When a therapist told them right off the bat that they weren't going to work, the couple tried to salvage their marriage. But Chris eventually stopped attending the sessions, and the author was advised to plan an exit strategy.

The author kept pushing her exit date back because she didn't want to jump into the separation so easily. Not long after, however, a girl disguised under the name 'Cameron Camera' would come into the picture. Chris and the author first met Cameron at a couples' potluck, wherein she was obviously trying to charm the married men. Chris hooked up with her shortly after --- once in the car, and another time in this office. And just as the author's new movie came out, Cameron revealed her big plan. She contacted tabloids saying she was ready to sell proof that the author's husband was cheating on her.

After the author's publicity team was informed about the rumor, the team did everything they could to make sure the wrong photos did not make it to the press. They hired a bodyguard, set up a sting, and put a price on the pictures. When her husband refused to own up to what he had done, their marriage was officially over. One night, the couple sat in bed together, talked things through calmly, and decided to split up. Because they had decided to talk before pushing through with the separation, they were able to somehow regain the friendship they had in the beginning.

The author ended up covering his expenses still, investing in his new company, helping him buy a car, and paying his rent. He soon squandered all those things, and never showed his face to her again.

11: Prescription for a Breakup

In this chapter, the author writes about the heartbreaks she has suffered throughout the years. From a bad breakup with her high school sweetheart, to pulling at all the stops so her boyfriend would break up with her, the author shares the biggest lessons she has learned about how to handle a break up, and how to come out a better woman.

She begins the chapter by laying out the plot of Warren Beatty and Natalie Wood's movie 'Splendor In The Grass', where Wood plays a woman heartbroken over her love's decision to sleep with another woman. She juxtaposes this with the way high school basketball star Jason Kidd broke up with her. At one of Jason's basketball games, she had noticed a girl in the bleachers wearing a wristband with his jersey number, while he wore one that read '#22', when the author's number was 21. After the game, Jason walked up to her, urged on by his friends, and told her that it was over. The author took the breakup really hard, and resorted to writing sad poetry about Jason afterwards.

Next on the list was the author's breakup with Alex, the boy she was with during the time of the Payless incident. After

Alex had dropped out of junior college, the author paid for his beauty school tuition with the money she got from the Payless settlement. However, he dropped out of beauty school as well. At this point, the author began to realize that the relationship wouldn't work if he did not match her ambition. It was here that she began to see a boy named Keith, who was a star soccer player and a law student. Although she and Keith hit it off, the author's plan was to cheat with Keith so that her current boyfriend Alex would break up with her.

Soon enough, Alex found out. Keith had sent a two page love letter to the author's house, mentioning their sexual endeavors, and Alex left. But the author wasn't very happy with Keith either, after realizing he was too boring for them to ever work. She searched around for information on Alex's whereabouts, and found out that he was now a backup dancer who was dating a model. The author writes about the time she staked out at Alex's new home in all-black clothing, peering in through his window.

She writes that all women have to go through times like this first, before they have their 'Angela Bassett Moment', or a moment wherein a woman finally realizes her self-worth. *"So, let Angela have it for you,"* she writes, *"breathe in the smoke from the car, and move on with her out of the bushes."*

For the rest of the chapter, she gives her readers more tips on how to handle the humiliation of a heartbreak, taking inspiration from Tina Turner finally finding the strength to continue with her divorce. She writes that after the period of craziness follows a satisfying drop, and eventually, things get better. In the author's words, *'You will fart your way to healing'*.

She ends this chapter by providing some more concrete tips on how to deal with a breakup: other men, and alcohol. She writes that women aren't required to have a 'healing period', or to abstain from sex after a breakup. Instead, they can meet other people as long as they are clear about their intentions of nor starting anything serious. Finally, she offers a list of drink pairings that can help through any situation. No matter what the booze is, she writes, the first round is on her.

12: On Mean Women and Good Dogs

The author begins this chapter with a few excerpts from her speech for *Essence* magazine, about being 'Fierce and Fearless'. Instead of including the usual Hollywood clichés about women empowerment, she instead decided to write about how she was not as fierce and fearless as everyone thought she was. She wrote about how much she felt like she needed to bring other people down just to make a name for herself in Hollywood, but that she later learned she only did it to hide from her own problems.

She writes about the time she hid under her bed after reaching a low point in life, with a divorce and a cancelled show. Her dog Bubba had law down right beside her under there, even though he was a large Mastiff Bulldog. She had gotten Bubba when he was a puppy, the runt of a six puppy litter. Bubba grew up to be very intuitive, especially with the author, and knew when she was in a bad place.

That was the moment the author decided to contact a life coach who had been prodding her to call for the longest time. The life coach, who she fondly called Coach, asked her to make a list of things that made her happy, and all she could think of were three food items. After two months, she finally completed a list of ten, and they began to unravel her way of thinking and her mental approach to life. At one party, the author found herself tearing down a fellow actress in front of an eager audience. Her Coach helped her realize that other people's pain was actually part of her Happy List. And that needed to change.

Following this, she writes about how being famous has really shown her how much society likes to revel in other people's pain and misfortune, for the sake of a mere moment of fame or visibility. She writes about learning to not obsess over negative comments written about her online, after a friend of hers says *"An empress does not concern herself with the antics of fools."*

Finally she pays homage to her best friend Bubba, who lived up to thirteen years old before passing away from kidney failure. *"He saw me at my worst and my meanest,"* she writes, *"and he loved me anyway."*

13: Warning: Famous Vaginas Get Itchy, Too

In this chapter, the author tells the story of the time she contracted a bad vaginal yeast infection, and let her fear of being exposed in a convenience store get in the way of getting proper medication.

She begins by writing about the moment wherein she urged her husband Dwyane to go into a supermarket and buy tampons for her. The reason for this, she writes, is that if she were to go in there, it would be the same as announcing her monthly flow to the world. But if Dwyane did, the media would find it cute that he was buying tampons for his wife.

She writes that this is only a glimpse of her thought process when it comes to purchasing something uncomfortable at a store. On a trip to Miami to see the man she was currently dating, the author felt a yeast infection coming. She attempted to get medicine at a nearby convenience store, but her plans were foiled when the store was packed, and everyone turned to look at her. She instead bought a pack of Twizzlers and walked out. After a friend suggested cranberry juice, she went back to the store to get Cran-Apple, which she later learned was pure sugar, and would only make her infection worse. Their next strategy was yogurt, but then she quickly realized she had no way of squeezing it up her vagina, unless she had a straw. Soon after, she found herself cutting the line at McDonald's to grab two Coke straws.

At the end of it all, the author realized that she was so afraid of being judged for having a yeast infection, a normal problem among women, that she put herself through a whole new set of humiliations. She writes,

"I resolved that that would be the last night
I found myself lying on some guy's kitchen floor
shoving yogurt up my hoohah. I would live a more authentic life."

14: Grown-Ass Woman Blues

In this chapter, the author revives sentiment from her previous chapters with similar titles, and talks about particular issues that come along when women reach a certain age. Here, she writes about the biggest moral dilemma of older working women across all industries: the decision of whether or not they should mentor younger women who are just starting out in the industry, or do everything they can to stop younger people from taking their jobs.

The author was first inspired to write about this 'grown-ass problem' after having lunch with two friends who were her age. At first, they shared thoughts about the struggle of getting a man at that age, when grown men are no longer interested and younger men just want to experiment. Even in different industries, grown-ass women live with the fear of being pushed over to make room for younger talents. The author's friend Michelle tells them about a young girl who just started at her company. She says that she can't stand her, and waves her friends off when they suggest that she help the young girl get settled into the company. Following this, the author starts to think about if she would take her own advice and mentor a younger actress.

She then tells the story of the first time she met young actress Ryan Destiny, who the press called 'The Next Gabrielle Union'. The press was spot-on, because Destiny looked like a carbon copy of her. Destiny had asked the author to be her mentor. *"Bitch, fuck you,"* she said in her head. The author felt threatened by a young actor who was already better than she was at that age, and was worried that as another actress won, she would lose.

Realizing her mistake, she writes that women who have worked longer in any industry had to drop this mentality, because being divided amongst each other made them a weaker force against the men who were favored in these industries. She writes,

"If I don't support and mentor someone like Ryan, that's working from a place of fear. And if I put my foot on a rising star, that's perpetuating a cycle that will keep us all weak."

15: Get Out Of My Pussy

In this chapter, the author writes about one thing the press hounds her the most about: her pregnancy, or the lack thereof. At the beginning of the chapter, she writes about a doctor's appointment in Miami where she was asked the question 'Are you pregnant?' repeatedly by various women, even though she had checked 'No' in the medical form. This was around the same time that there were rumors circulating in the tabloids about her being pregnant again. She is in shock about how clickbait articles have affected even her medical care.

Following this, she writes about her struggle to have a baby with her husband Dwyane. She has had about eight or nine miscarriages, and talks about why they keep trying despite coming up short several times. She writes, *"This child we want to have has been loved even as an idea. Each attempt at IVF is a loving action."*

The author then talks about how different people have reacted or responded to her fertility issues. She would constantly get invited to baby showers and her friends would send her cute pictures of their own babies, in order to keep the author's hope alive about having a successful pregnancy.

At one baby shower, the expecting mother, who also originally had trouble conceiving, told her that she finally succeeded at conceiving when she quit her job and focused on having a baby.

The author doesn't see this as an option. She is determined to make her own income despite having a wealthy husband, and is tired of the notion that women have to give up one aspect of their lives just to do well in everything else. She writes about how she has been asked questions regarding her pregnancy on numerous occasions, to the point where she told one reporter that until they started asking her husband the same questions, she wouldn't answer any more. This is in line with a long time issue in the Hollywood scene, wherein men are asked substantial interview questions, while women have to tell reporters about what they eat to stay in such great shape. The author's only real answer to the never ending pregnancy inquiries is *"Get Out Of My Pussy! Just. Get. The. Fuck. Out."*

16: And Gabrielle Union As… The Stepmother

In this chapter, the author writes about being a stepmother two her husband Dwyane's two sons and nephew, Zion, the youngest at nine, fifteen year old Zaire, and sixteen year old Dada. She writes about the motions a stepmother has to go through, what a stepmother has to keep in mind, and being a parent to children as though they are one's own. Beyond this, she writes about what it's really like to be a parent to three black children whose privilege cannot always save them from the discrimination they might face on the streets.

She begins the chapter by writing about the mindset she had during the first few months of being a stepmother to the three boys. She writes that the key to being a good stepparent is to be consistent, meaning it is never a good idea to try and be best friends with the children one day and be a disciplinarian the next. She also notes that another important thing to remember is that no child wants their mother replaced, and it's important for a stepparent to know which lines should not be crossed.

Following this, the author shares the story of how Dwayne proposed to her, and how the three boys were part of the proposal. They had held up a sign saying "Will you marry us?" in front of the author, and once she turned, Dwyane was on his knees asking the same question. She writes that what felt so good about this moment was that she knew she wasn't crashing into a family, and that they were actually welcoming her into it.

She then begins to talk about the struggle of being a present parent and working at the same time, in the case of her and her husband alike. With every missed school event and tournament, she felt as though she was failing them. Even more so, she wanted to fight the stereotype of black mothers being disciplinarians, bent on teaching their children independence, instead wanting to be seen as nurturing, a trait often ascribed to white mothers.

It is at this point that she writes about how she has gone about raising her black sons in a way that they are aware of their odds. She writes, *"Black Bombs are what I call the inescapable truths of being a black person in this country, the things you do your children a disservice by not telling them about."*

She drops a Black Bomb on Zaire and Dada as they are about to sleep over at a friend's house, reminding them to not wander around, so that no one can accuse them of stealing. She recalls talking to them multiple times about not talking back to authority figures or being violent in school, because regardless of their status, their bodies would always be easy to label with words like 'thug' or 'delinquent'. On one occasion, the author was called to the principal's office after Zaire had 'bullied' a fellow student. She writes that she brought spreadsheets and reference books to the meeting, in order to help her point out that when a white student had called her son a 'nigger', the matter was dismissed as a case of *'Boys will be boys'*. On the contrary, her son was called a bully.

She drops another Black bomb when her two older sons ask to play at a nearby basketball gym, to which the friend who owned it had given the author and Dwyane the keys to. It was already dark out and they lived in a rich neighborhood, or rather, the type of neighborhood that would alert the police if they saw two black bodies 'lurking' the streets late at night. In spite of her efforts to avoid this, her husband allowed them to go when they asked again the next night.

Once the author talked sense into her husband, they jumped into a golf cart and followed the boys to the gym. The author had called up her son, who told her that the keys didn't work, and that they were on their way back, when a police car passed by the author and her husband. The car stopped upon coming in contact with them, and drove off when her husband introduced himself. She recalls telling her husband,

"If you think these cops were not called on our boys, you are fucking delusional."

She recalls an incident from the year before, when the two boys were walking the family dog around the neighborhood. The police were present in the area because of a prank done on a celebrity's house nearby, and as more and more police cars passed, the boys froze on the side of the road, thinking the cars were coming for them. One car stopped at where they were, and out of fear, Zaire dropped the dog's leash and he and Dada started to run back to the house. They had no idea what to do in that type of situation, despite their mother coaching them about it for years. As the boys told her and her husband the story, almost laughingly, the author recalls telling them they could have been shot in the back.

17: Mittens

In this chapter, the writer shares two stories --- one of her own, and one of a close friend's --- which share a similar lesson: when black people are spotted in a place their kind usually aren't supposed to be, their every move is questioned, and their doubters will do anything before admitting it is because they are black.

The author begins the chapter by providing the events that would lead up to her realization. When her husband started playing for the Chicago Bulls, they moved into a house on the Gold Coast, the most expensive neighborhood in the city. She recalls walking to the gym every morning and watching the neighbors wonder who she is, and from the looks on their faces, who she works for. One day before her walk, she decided to put on a pair of mittens along with layers of clothing in the hopes of seeming less frightening to the neighbors. However, despite the mittens, she still felt terrified of what other people would think when they saw her walking along a muddy path.

Following this, she tells the story of her friend Ricky Williams, a retired Miami Doplhin, and his run-in with the police. Walking in the vicinity of his hotel room before an awards ceremony, he was stopped by some police officers who had been notified of a 'suspicious' man. As he was being questioned, ordered to put his hands up, and was about to be searched, one officer recognized him as Ricky Williams. After this discovery, the cops became unsure of what the next step was. While they knew he wasn't guilty of anything, they still had to follow protocol. When Ricky mentioned how often he has been stopped by police officers, the cops acted like it was preposterous for him to even think it was about race.

She writes that the police were offended by this notion because people tend to get annoyed when the 'race card' is played. She expresses that while these kinds of incidents came as no surprise to black people, their stories still deserved to be heard, because it only proves further that the idea of 'making it' as a black person never means safety. She recalls people of color telling her to not make everything about race, believing that they have become successful enough to not have their skin color define them. These people believed a person could choose to be defined by their skin color, or choose to be defined by their 'humanness'. The author disagrees with this. A person could be humane and still be stopped by the police for being black. She writes,

'My humanness doesn't insulate me from racism or sexism.
In fact, I think I can deal effectively with the world precisely because

I am a black woman who is so comfortable in my black-womanness. I know what I can accomplish. And anything I have accomplished, I did so not in spite of being a black woman, but because I am a black woman."

18: Big Bank Take Little Bank

The author begins this chapter with a glimpse into her and her husband's favorite televisions show, *Nashville*. She writes about the storyline of Deacon and Rayna, who play lovers on the show. The author writes that one thing that has always drawn her to their story is the fact that Rayna was the one earning more in the relationship. She relates this to her experiences with past marriages and relationships, where she was the one who paid for everything, but that in her marriage with Dwyane, she was Deacon.

Although Dwyane is loaded, the author has one house in Los Angeles that she pays for by herself. The disparity of their incomes had even become a source of humor for the couple. The author writes that sometimes Dwyane would forget his wallet on purpose when they went out to eat, just so she could pay. She stresses that even in a marriage where everything is supposed to be shared, the partner with a higher income always somehow has the upper hand.

The author writes about what had transpired when she and her husband arranged for a prenup before their marriage. While the author had initially wanted to leave the marriage, if she had to, with whatever she came with, Dwyane's team insisted on giving her a share of his money after. She began to feel that the prenup was practically evaluating her and determining her worth. Her team had been trying to increase her 'worth' by listing down her past work and fame, while Dwyane's team was telling them she was worth less. In the end, she signed the deal.

She writes that she is still resentful about how the prenup went, but that her and Dwyane's wedding solidified the love they had for each other, not as big and little banks, but as people who loved each other without conditions. She closes the chapter with excerpts from their wedding vows.

"If you've ever wondered if I'll leave you, the answer is never,"
Dwyane said to me in front of all those people.
"And if you've ever wondered what I value, the answer is you."

19: The Room Where It Happens

In this story, the author pays tribute to one particular star who impacted her life and career in many ways, through his infectious energy, strong spirituality, and unmatched power to unite people from every corner of Hollywood in spite of the divisions that exist within the industry. The author writes about Prince.

The first time she was invited to a Prince part was in 2005. She received a text from an unknown number telling her the location of the party that was happening on the same night the messages were sent out. Upon arriving at the venue, she immediately saw a trio of big stars --- Whitney Houston, Mariah Carey, and Mary J. Blige gossiping in one corner of the room. Although she was starstruck upon meeting many celebrities that night, she was most anxious and eager about meeting Prince. When she had expressed surprise over him recognizing her from *The ER*, Prince had remarked *"I see everything."* And he did. The author writes that he really did see everyone, from the biggest stars to the writers and producers behind it all.

Following this, she writes that the reason why she marveled at Prince's party was because segregation exists within

Hollywood. Since the stars who become your friends are the same people you are in the audition room with for a film looking to give a black actress a few speaking lines, black actors and actresses hung out with other black actresses. But despite building a community among themselves, the author expresses they are still not allowed into the room where bigger things happen. She writes that even after brown actors are invited to Golden Ticket events, they still feel like interlopers, and find safety in the company of other brown actors.

She writes about the controversy of award shows like the Oscars being whitewashed, because award-winning white directors cast famous white actors, and the cycle goes on. *"We all know you can create even better art by truly being inclusive,"* she writes, *"but you're never going to get inclusive in your work if you can't figure out how to get inclusive in your social life."* Prince was one of the people who didn't stick to the status quo, and threw parties with all kinds of people.

The author writes more about the friendship we formed with Prince. During a small dinner party Prince hosted, he talked to his guests a lot about spirituality. He confided in the author that there was always a 'religious component' to his parties, because he wanted to see what unites people.

The author even talks about how she owes Prince her marriage, because she had met Dwyane's younger brother at one of Prince's parties. The brother then asked if she was willing to cohost a party in Miami, where the author would eventually meet her husband. She talked about how devastated her husband was after learning of Prince's death. Even though he didn't know Prince like his wife did, Prince had said in an interview that Dwyane Wade was his favorite player.

After the legend's death, more and more news came out about Prince's elaborate parties. The author noted that none of these articles mentioned the brown people who were at the party. While she writes that she mourns for Prince as an icon in music, she grieves just as much for the loss of someone who had brought so many people together. At the end of the story, she writes that she had always wanted to ask Prince one question: *"What is it you see in me? That maybe I am not seeing in myself?"*

20: A Tale Of Two Martinezes

In this final chapter, the author writes about two of the closest friends she has ever had, and how their stories shaped her own experiences and determined what cause she would be fighting for the rest of her life. From these two Martinezes, she learned one very important lesson, which she also mentioned in the introduction to this book: that one can be afraid, but at the same time strong enough to do what needs to be done anyway.

The author met the first Martinez, a dance-loving classmate named Ray, when he literally volunteered to be her friend at the start of the school year. United by their love of song and dance, they would go to different cities during class hours just to buy more dance music. Ray had a sister, fondly called Sookie, who the author quickly connected with as well. Even though others would call Ray a 'fag' or 'gay' under their breath, the author never suspected he was a homosexual. She recalls Sookie showing up with a bloody Ray at her front door, after someone had called Ray 'a bad name'.

While she bonded with Ray over music, the author bonded with Sookie over their love for black boys. They would wear matching outfits and go to an all-ages club where black boys would hang out, and have the time of their lives. Both Martinezes became her best friends. Both of them showed her a life beyond the smallness of Pleasanton.

Ray would always tell the author and her friends that he wanted to move to San Francisco one day. Although he never said why, he would later learn it was because he wanted to be with his people. At one party, some kids had called Ray a faggot, and the author jumped in to protect him, screaming, "He is not a fucking faggot!". She realizes later on that she did not do this to protect him; she only felt that outsiders like them could not afford any more reasons to be the "other". She was stopping Ray from being who he really was.

At a high school reunion party, she was the last person to find out that Ray was a homosexual. Ray opened up to her about being hurt every time she said the word 'fag' in front of him, and the author realized how wrong she had been. She writes, "*I was too busy protecting our spots on a Jenga tower of assimilationist bullshit to be the friend he needed.*"

Meanwhile, Sookie and the author only reconnected when they ran into each other one night in Las Vegas. It was here that Sookie told her about the lump in her breast, and that by the time she had it checked, her metastatic breast cancer was already at Stage Four. Immediately, the author was determined to help her fix it. She hooked Sookie up with the best doctors she knew, found ways to get the amount she needed to see those doctors, and became involved in breast cancer foundations that landed her at a breast cancer facility in Ghana. During a speech by an expert on breast cancer, she finally learned what 'metastatic' meant after years of putting off research on it. Metastatic breast cancer was incurable.

After this discovery, the author dedicated her efforts to spending as much time with Sookie as possible. While they ate lunch in a New York restaurant, the author asked Sookie what she wanted her legacy to be. She recalls her best friend saying, *"I want you to tell people that fear can kill you. I was afraid, and it killed me."*

She was right there with the rest of Sookie's family on one of her last nights. Sookie was asking for hair removal cream and nail polish, wanting to look as pretty as possible in her last moments. After Sookie died that same week, she writes that what Sookie wanted other people to know was that they needed to prioritize their health and wellbeing. Asking an opinion from the doctor was an integral part of living one's best life.

Despite not being able to save Sookie, the author continued to advocate for breast cancer awareness and research, and has been very active in supporting Planned Parenthood. At the end of the chapter, she has a single message to the readers she took along with her on the journey of telling these stories:

Take care of yourself.

Conclusion

Gabrielle Union's twenty stories felt nothing like a first date. Instead, it felt like a record-holder for the longest marriage. Staying true to the description of her book, *'Stories that are fun, complicated, and true'*, the author took her readers through the funniest, lowest, and most heartwarming parts of what has been her life, leaving them awestruck at her candidness and wisdom.

In one of her stories, she writes that she has achieved success and happiness in life not in spite of her being a black woman, but rather, because of this. And she proves this time and time again with each story she tells. She never once lets go of her identity as a black woman. She never takes it out of the equation. She allows it to define her in the most elegant and fearless of ways. The way she writes about black oppression and discrimination in a way that is nothing short of intelligent, in that she acknowledges the issue is multi-faceted, yet very simple at the same time. She knows better than to think herself above it because she has 'made it'. Her stories all bear the lesson that issues regarding her skin color still very much exist in her world just as much as they did when she was a young black girl in Pleasanton.

Gabrielle Union's stories are the stories of a woman of color who is not only proud of where her blackness has gotten her, but has also equipped herself with the knowledge of her own odds, through books she has read and moments she has lived. It is this knowledge that allows her to continue to be aware of the inequalities that exist in the world. It is this knowledge that now protects her sons and the people she loves. But what is equally apparent is that she never attempts to hide how she has let herself be held back by the fear of being 'othered' as well, whether it's when she used mittens to make her black body seem less suspicious, or when she hurt a close friend because she didn't want to further endanger their standing in the social hierarchy.

At the end of the day, the author's stories are the stories of a woman who has learned how to succeed with the tools, traits and talents she had been given from the start. She prepared herself for what she would face but tried her hardest not to let the fear of these stop her from doing it anyway. Women of all ages and backgrounds are able to see themselves in the moments she shares, and have maybe even had the same realizations after. While her stories are speckled with shining Hollywood stars and souls from an entirely different part of the world, it teaches the same lesson every person must be taught at one point in their lives. People continue to

learn about who they are through the hearts of other people they meet along the way. It is a lifelong process of uncovering the best and worst parts of oneself, and of finding oneself in places one never expects.

Final Thoughts

Hey! Did you enjoy this book? We sincerely hope you thoroughly enjoyed this short read and have gotten immensely valuable insights that will help you in any areas of your life.

Would it be too greedy if we ask for a review from you?

It takes 1 minute to leave 1 review to possibly influence 1 more person's decision to read just 1 book which may change their 1 life. Your 1 minute matters and we value it and thank you so much for giving us your 1 minute. If it sucks, just say it sucks. Period.

FREE BONUS

P.S. Is it okay if we overdeliver?

Here at Abbey Beathan Publishing, we believe in overdelivering way beyond our reader's expectations. Is it okay if we overdeliver?

Here's the deal, we're going to give you an extremely valuable cheatsheet of "Accelerated Learning". We've partnered up with Ikigai Publishing to present to you the exclusive bonus of "Accelerated Learning Cheatsheet"

What's the catch? We need to trust you… You see, we want to overdeliver and in order for us to do that, we've to trust our reader to keep this bonus a secret to themselves. Why? Because we don't want people to be getting our exclusive accelerated learning cheatsheet without even buying our books itself. Unethical, right?

Ok. Are you ready?

Simply Visit this link: http://bit.ly/acceleratedcheatsheet

We hope you'll enjoy our free bonuses as much as we've enjoyed preparing it for you!

Free Bonus #2: Free Book Preview of Summary: Fat for Fuel

The Book at a Glance

The book focuses on the use of Mitochondrial Metabolic Therapy (MMT) to attain a healthy body. This particular technique aims to help in repairing and maintaining the proper functioning of the mitochondria. Mitochondrial dysfunction is seen as a cause of many diseases because of the release of reactive oxygen species (ROS) and the inability to promote apoptosis.

Research has revealed that high carb diets have a negative effect on this organelle, causing abnormalities in the various metabolic processes. Given that the modern American diet has become synonymous with highly processed carbohydrates, it isn't surprising at all that many end up experiencing mitochondrial aberrations. Thus, it's the aim of MMT to promote health by establishing guidelines and strategies that will ensure that the mitochondria stay in tiptop shape.

In the book's first part, the basic principles concerning the mitochondria, free radicals, and MMT are explained in detail. It also discusses the high fat, low carb diet that is recommended for MMT practitioners. Note that Part 1 is divided into five chapters. Chapter 1 focuses on the nature of the mitochondria as an organelle and its ability to produce free radicals. Chapter 2 deals with the reasons to undergo MMT. Chapter 3 talks about the use of protein and the dangers of having them in excess. Chapter 4 covers the use of iron in the body and its adverse effects (when present in great amounts). Chapter 5 deals with the diet involved in MMT.

Part 2 of the book explains the do's and don'ts of MMT. It's filled with guidelines and tips for a successful practice of MMT's principles. This part is divided into six chapters. Chapter 6 provides details on the preparation phase before undergoing MMT. Chapter 7 discusses the things that must be done upon starting MMT. Chapter 8 talks about transitioning from glucose to fat as the main source of energy for the body. Chapter 9 gives advice on how to stick with MMT for the long-term, while chapter 10 explains the importance of fasting and the proper ways to do it. Finally, Chapter 11 talks about other ways to help repair and maintain the mitochondria.

Each chapter of the book contains examples given by doctors. Actual health problems are tackled and readers are motivated by true success stories. Scientific evidence is used throughout the book, even those not directly related to the mitochondria but have an impact nonetheless. Without a doubt, the book finds ways to encourage the reader to adopt MMT for better health and a more fulfilling life.

Introduction

Joseph Mercola's early fitness lifestyle was highly influenced by his fondness of *Aerobics* — a book that, as some would say, eventually led him to go to medical school. Although he was technically involved in mainstream science (particularly in fitness and health), he was still intrigued by the most popular health fads of his time. He was particularly interested in the low-fat, high-carb diet that was actually doing more harm than good.

He eventually met Dr. Ron Rosedale and became interested in the critical need to control high insulin levels in order to prevent nearly every chronic degenerative disease. These diseases (which include diabetes, obesity, heart disease, cancer, arthritis, and neurodegenerative disorders) have become rampant these days. The author also read Travis Christofferson's *Tripping over the Truth: How the Metabolic Theory of Cancer Is Overturning One of Medicine's Most Entrenched Paradigms*. He then realized that chronic diseases and cancer emerge because of mitochondrial dysfunction, which actually creates limitations in the metabolic processes. Leptin and insulin receptors develop resistance because carbohydrates are taken in excessive amounts. Likewise, mammalian target of rapamycin (mTOR) signaling is activated because of too much protein intake. What happens when mTOR signaling occurs far too frequently? Tumors develop.

The mitochondrion is known as the powerhouse of the cell and its job is to convert nutrients (especially carbohydrates) coupled with oxygen into ATP or energy. This particular organelle can also cause living systems to function abnormally or not at all if it becomes dysfunctional. This is an important point of view when it comes to the study of cancer cells. Now, if a disease like cancer can start because of organelle dysfunction, then it can be stopped if that organelle is repaired. This is the objective of the author. He wants to educate the people in the possible techniques that can be done to help prevent and stop cancer and other related illnesses.

The author hypothesized that it all starts with the type of food eaten every day. A change in diet, from one that's loaded with carbohydrates into one that features high quality fats, will create massive changes to health and fitness.

To further learn about nutrition and its effects on the human body, the author met with Miriam Kalamian — a nutrition consultant, educator, and author. The two discussed the implementation of ketogenic therapies for people with cancer, putting emphasis on the importance of ketones in repairing the mitochondria and preventing cancer. Now, Miriam is the nutrition consultant for Dr. Thomas Seyfried, who is widely recognized as one of the leading pioneers in the metabolic theory of cancer.

All things considered, the author's goal is to provide a concise, clear, and scientific explanation about the effect of diet on the normal functioning of the mitochondria and the treatment of cancer cells. That's why *Fat for Fuel* gives a list of things to eat, convenient techniques to follow, and practical ways to track the things you're going to do in improving your mitochondrial health — collectively, this program is called Mitochondrial Metabolic Therapy (MMT). Again, MMT is composed of a diet regimen that changes the metabolism's reliance on sugar, shifting its attention towards the use of fat in producing the energy needed by the body. This shift will optimize the abilities of the mitochondria and will also protect the DNA from possible abnormalities.

The MMT diet is high in fat, moderate in protein, and low in carbohydrates. As you've probably noticed, this is considerably different from what is deemed normal by the American public. The usual American diet is composed of a lot of refined grains, processed sugar-loaded products, and low-quality fat. The MMT diet is actually more delicious and satisfying. It takes away hunger, cravings, and any feelings of deprivation. It also provides a noticeable energy boost. Aside from being beneficial to those already suffering from neurodegenerative disease (like Alzheimer's and dementia), cancer, type-2 diabetes, and obesity, MMT helps people who are looking to improve their overall health while slowing down the aging process.

The author puts emphasis on the number of studies showing the importance of mitochondrial health in metabolic health. At some point in the future, this different kind of therapy will be accepted as a standard for taking care of patients with cancer and most other chronic diseases.

Read More…

SUMMARY
FAT FOR FUEL
A REVOLUTIONARY DIET TO COMBAT CANCER, BOOST BRAIN POWER, AND INCREASE YOUR ENERGY
BY: DR. JOSEPH MERCOLA
ABBEY BEATHAN

CPSIA information can be obtained
at www.ICGtesting.com
Printed in the USA
LVHW042118280619
622739LV00001B/19/P

9 781646 154104